SWITZERLAND

Lyn Larson

Lerner Publications Company • Minneapolis

Lerner Publications Company
A division of Lerner Publishing Group, Inc.
241 First Avenue North
Minneapolis, MN 55401 U.S.A.

Website address: www.lernerbooks.com

Library of Congress Cataloging-in-Publication Data

Larson, Lyn.
    Switzerland / by Lyn Larson.
        p.   cm. — (Country explorers)
    Includes index.
    ISBN 978-0-7613-6418-4 (lib. bdg. : alk. paper)
    1. Switzerland—Juvenile literature. I. Title.
DQ17.L37 2012
949.4—dc22   2010046742

Manufactured in the United States of America
1 – PP – 7/15/11

SWITZERLAND

COUNTRY EXPLORERS

Lyn Larson

Lerner Publications Company • Minneapolis

Lerner Publications Company
A division of Lerner Publishing Group, Inc.
241 First Avenue North
Minneapolis, MN 55401 U.S.A.

Website address: www.lernerbooks.com

Library of Congress Cataloging-in-Publication Data

Larson, Lyn.
    Switzerland / by Lyn Larson.
        p.   cm. — (Country explorers)
    Includes index.
    ISBN 978-0-7613-6418-4 (lib. bdg. : alk. paper)
    1. Switzerland—Juvenile literature. I. Title.
DQ17.L37 2012
949.4—dc22   2010046742

Manufactured in the United States of America
1 – PP – 7/15/11

Table of Contents

Welcome!

Let's go to Switzerland! This country sits on the continent of Europe. Five countries surround Switzerland. Germany lies to the north. Liechtenstein and Austria are to the east. Italy shares Switzerland's southern border. And France sits to the west.

North Sea

Switzerland

Mediterranean Sea

equator

The small village of Riom lies in the Swiss Alps.

N

GERMANY

FRANCE

LIECHTENSTEIN

AUSTRIA

ITALY

FRANCE

RHINE RIVER

REUSS RIVER

Lake Constance

Zurich

Lake Zurich

RHINE RIVER

JURA MOUNTAINS

SWISS PLATEAU

Lucerne

SWITZERLAND

Bern

AARE RIVER

Mathon

SWISS ALPS

TICINO RIVER

Lake Geneva

RHONE RIVER

Geneva

THE MATTERHORN

Zermatt

MILES

0   10   20   30   40

0   20   40   60

KILOMETERS

mountains

central plateau

★ country's capital

• city

The Swiss Alps have steep, jagged peaks.

Surrounded by Mountains

Switzerland has lots of mountains. The largest mountain range in Europe is the Alps. These mountains cover more than half of Switzerland.

The Jura mountain range forms Switzerland's western border. These mountains are not as high as the Alps. Between the two mountain ranges lies the flat Swiss Plateau. The rich farmland here is good for raising crops and animals.

Many crops grow on the Swiss Plateau. This farmer cuts down hay. It will be fed to cattle.

7

The ice of this glacier looks blue.

Glaciers, Lakes, and Rivers

The Swiss Alps are an important source of fresh water. Lots of snow falls in the mountains. Glaciers are huge sheets of ice. They lie between mountain peaks. In spring, the snow and ice melt. The water flows into lakes and rivers.

Two important rivers start in the Swiss Alps. The Rhine River flows to the North Sea. The Rhone River runs southeast to the Mediterranean Sea. Switzerland has more than fourteen hundred lakes. The largest one is Lake Geneva.

Clean Energy

Rivers provide an important source of energy. More than five hundred power plants use the rushing water to make electricity.

This small lake in the Swiss Alps is the start of the Rhone River.

Weather Differences

What's the weather like where you live? Winters are cold and snowy in the Alps. Most of the high peaks stay below freezing all year-round. On the slopes, summers are cool. The slopes and lower peaks receive lots of rain.

Snow covers the village of Zermatt in winter. The nearby Matterhorn mountain is one of the highest peaks in the Swiss Alps.

10

In lower areas, temperatures are warmer. Summer temperatures range from 65 to 82°F (18 to 28°C). The Swiss Plateau gets less rain. But mountain rivers bring water to this area.

In summer, people enjoy boating on Lake Zurich.

Swiss Animals

Switzerland's mountains are home to several kinds of animals. Ibex are small, wild goats. Males have huge horns that curve back past their necks.

In the Alps, the ibex was hunted until nearly extinct. It is now a protected animal.

Chamois are relatives of goats and antelope. They are larger than ibex. But their horns are shorter.

Saint Bernards

The first Saint Bernard dogs lived with people in the Swiss mountains. These huge dogs could push through deep snow. They made paths for people to walk. They also rescued people trapped in snow.

A chamois has brown fur in the summer and gray fur in the winter.

From War to Peace

Long ago, people from many backgrounds lived in what became modern-day Switzerland. Faraway rulers controlled the area for hundreds of years. Local people started their own government in the late 1200s. They called it the Swiss Confederation.

The founding members of the Swiss Confederation take their oath in 1291.

The Swiss army won many battles to gain more land. But in the 1500s, Swiss leaders decided to stop fighting. They also chose not to take sides in other countries' battles. Switzerland became a peaceful country.

The Red Cross

A Swiss man named Jean Henri Dunant started the Red Cross in 1863. This group helps people during wars and natural disasters. It has volunteers around the world.

Soldiers stand at attention in Bern. The army takes part in peacekeeping missions around the world.

Many Cultures Together

About seven million people live in Switzerland. More than half have German backgrounds. Others have French and Italian ancestors.

This house in Lucerne is painted in a German style. People in this city speak German.

16

A small group has Romansh backgrounds. Their ancestors came from ancient Rome. They speak Romansh. It is an old language based on Latin.

Mathon is a Romansh-speaking village in the Swiss Alps.

Major Cities

About three out of every four Swiss people live in a city. The largest city is Zurich. Zurich is famous for its banks.

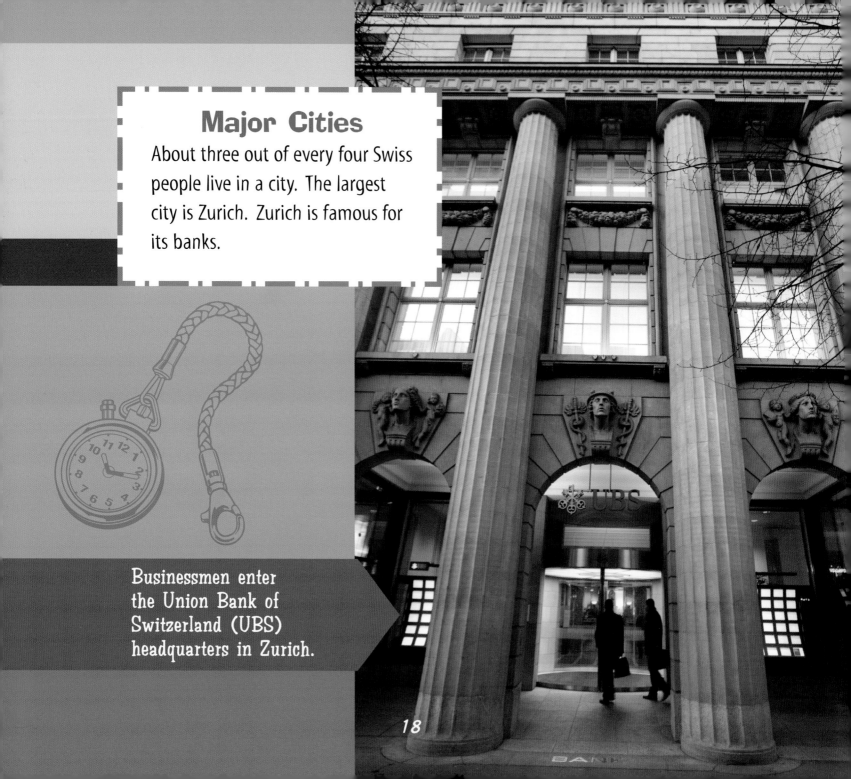

Businessmen enter the Union Bank of Switzerland (UBS) headquarters in Zurich.

18

Geneva is the second-largest city. This city is called the
capital of peace. The United Nations has offices here.
This group brings together leaders from many countries.

Bern

Dear Grandma and Grandpa,
Today we are visiting Bern, Switzerland's
capital. This city's name means "bear."
And people here are bear crazy! You can
watch real bears play at an outdoor park.
Bear sculptures sit in fountains. Even the
city's flag has a bear on it. Bern is also
where they make Toblerone chocolate
bars. And guess what? A picture of a
bear is hidden on the candy's label!
See you soon!
Haley

A

Made in Switzerland

The Swiss are famous for their watches. A Swiss company made one of the first wristwatches in 1868. The Swiss also invented the first waterproof watch. They even created a watch that works on the moon. The Swiss are also good at making electrical equipment, machinery, and tools.

A man uses a magnifying glass to examine the inside of a Swiss watch.

Swiss Army Knives

Swiss Army knives have tools that fold into the handle. The earliest Swiss Army knives included a knife blade, a screwdriver, a can opener, and a hole punch. Over time, makers added more tools, such as a scissors, a saw blade, and even a fork and a spoon.

This Swiss army knife features a knife blade, a can opener, a saw, a scissors, and other tools.

21

Family Life

How many brothers and sisters do you have? Swiss families usually have one or two children. In most families, fathers have full-time jobs. Many mothers work part-time. They are able to spend more time with their children.

This Swiss family has a pet goat.

Swiss families enjoy time outdoors. In summer, parents take kids hiking or swimming. During winter, many people go downhill or cross-country skiing.

Hiking is a popular pastime for many Swiss families.

23

Homes

Only one in three Swiss people owns a house. Most people live in cities. Some buy condos, while others rent apartments.

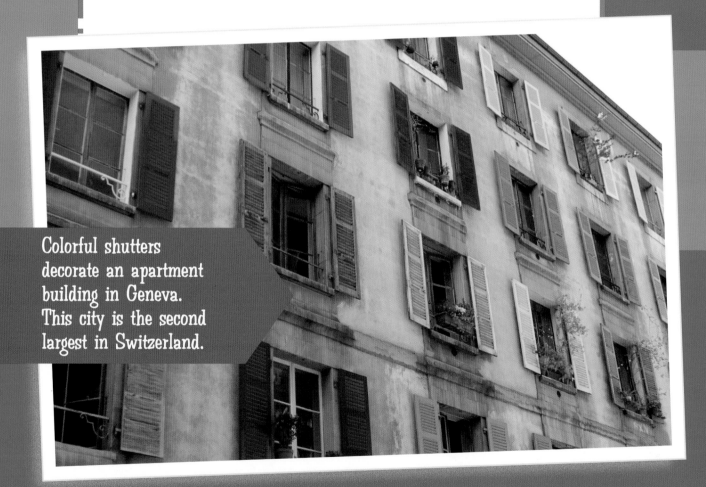

Colorful shutters decorate an apartment building in Geneva. This city is the second largest in Switzerland.

In rural areas, many people own chalets. A chalet has a large roof that stretches past the walls of the house. The top floors have balconies and flower boxes.

Flowers bloom in window boxes on this chalet.

Cheese and Chocolate

Have you eaten Swiss cheese? It has holes in it. Fondue is a popular dish. Cooks make fondue with melted Swiss cheeses. People dip chunks of bread into fondue.

Swiss cheeses come in many varieties.

The Swiss are also famous for their chocolate. Swiss food makers created the first bars of milk chocolate. The Swiss also made the first chocolate candy with fillings.

An employee puts chocolates in boxes at a factory.

Chocolate Lovers

The Swiss eat more chocolate than people in any other country. On average, each person in Switzerland eats about 25 pounds (11 kilograms) each year!

Getting Around

Switzerland's mountains make travel tricky. But the country has a good system of roads, railways, and waterways. Many roads and railways run through tunnels in mountains. The tunnels are shortcuts.

A passenger train passes over the tallest rock bridge in Switzerland.

Buses, trains, and airplanes
also help people to travel.
Most people own cars as well.

This city bus in Geneva helps
many people travel to work.

Two elementary school students work together in a classroom.

Schooltime

Swiss kids go to school from about the ages of six to fifteen. The school year runs from September to June. Swiss students study geography, history, math, and science. Classes are taught in the main language of the area.

After grade nine, students decide whether to go to high school or to learn a trade. Kids who go to high school can go to a university or to another advanced school.

Art students create an outdoor sculpture using clear plastic bags.

gesperrt

barrée

chiusa

closed

This sign uses four different languages to tell people that a ski run is closed.

Four National Languages

Switzerland's four national languages are German, French, Italian, and Romansh. People speak the language of their area. They usually learn one other national language too. Some people also learn English.

Good Words to Know

English	German	French	Italian	Romansh
hello	guten Tag	bonjour	ciao	allegra
please	bitte	s'il vous plait	per favore	per plaschair
thank you	danke schön	merci	grazie	grazia fitg
yes	ja	oui	si	gea
no	nein	non	no	na
good-bye	auf Wiedersehen	adieu	arrivederci	a revair

Swiss newspapers offer a choice of languages.

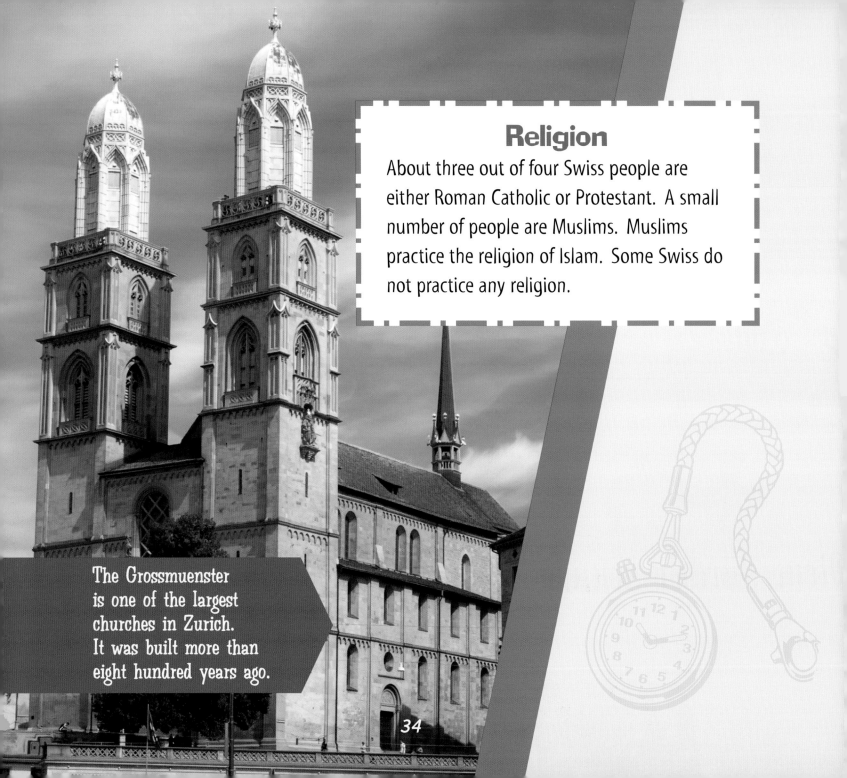

Religion

About three out of four Swiss people are either Roman Catholic or Protestant. A small number of people are Muslims. Muslims practice the religion of Islam. Some Swiss do not practice any religion.

The Grossmuenster is one of the largest churches in Zurich. It was built more than eight hundred years ago.

During the 1500s, Roman Catholics and Protestants had many battles. Later, the government wrote laws so people would respect all religions.

In the 1540s, John Calvin (*standing*) worked with other leaders in Geneva to reform the church laws. His ideas started a new Protestant religion called Calvinism.

Celebrate!

Do you like celebrations? So do the Swiss. People honor Swiss National Day on August 1. This marks the date when Switzerland became a country in 1291. People enjoy torchlight parades, fireworks, and bonfires.

Families enjoy watching parades on Swiss National Day. Marchers wear traditional clothing and carry regional flags.

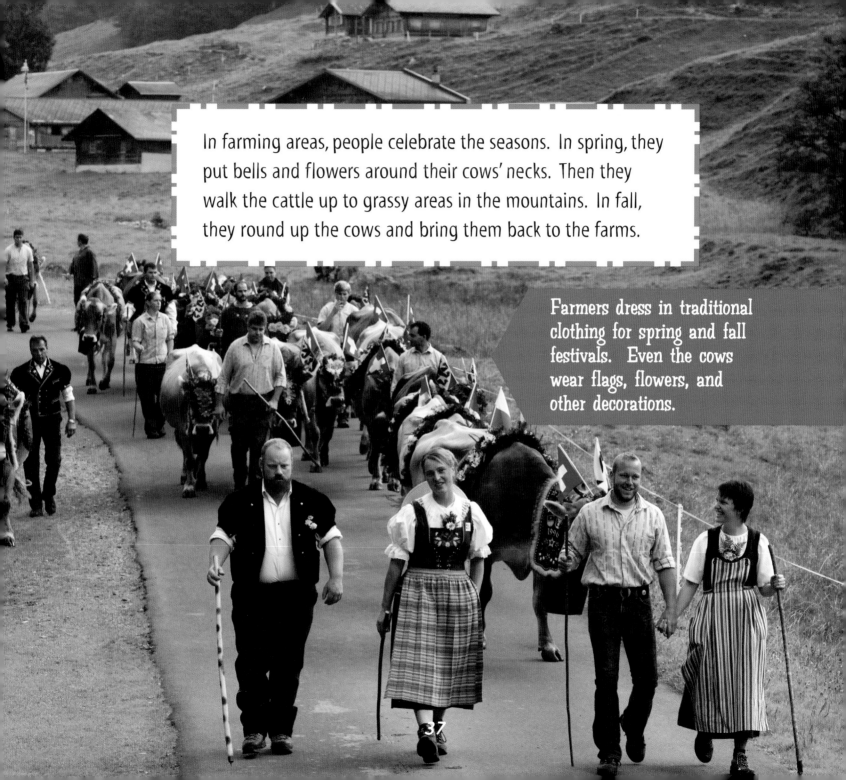

In farming areas, people celebrate the seasons. In spring, they put bells and flowers around their cows' necks. Then they walk the cattle up to grassy areas in the mountains. In fall, they round up the cows and bring them back to the farms.

Farmers dress in traditional clothing for spring and fall festivals. Even the cows wear flags, flowers, and other decorations.

Stories and Legends

Have you read the book *Heidi*? It is about a girl who lives in the Swiss mountains. Author Johanna Spyri wrote the story in 1880. The book has been translated into more than fifty languages. It also inspired many movies, TV shows, and plays.

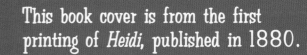

This book cover is from the first printing of *Heidi*, published in 1880.

William Tell is a Swiss legend. In this story, an evil ruler puts William Tell in prison. To get out, William has to shoot an apple off his son's head. If his arrow misses, both he and his son will die. William makes the shot and outsmarts the ruler. This legend inspires many people during hard times.

This engraving shows William Tell shooting an apple off his son's head.

A Love for Music

The Swiss enjoy all kinds of music. Many Swiss cities have outdoor concerts. The music ranges from classical to rock, pop, and jazz.

More than 200,000 people come to see the Paléo Festival. It is the second-largest outdoor music event in mainland Europe.

Yodeling is a style of folk singing that came from mountain areas. Yodelers suddenly change from high to low notes and back again. Long ago, people sang this way to gather cattle and call over distances.

Long Winded

Musicians play the alphorn at many special events. This wooden instrument is up to 12 feet (3 m) long. People change notes with their lips and breath. The music travels long distances in the mountains.

Three men play alphorns by blowing into the instruments.

41

Sports and Activities

Soccer is called football in Switzerland. The game is the most popular national sport. The Swiss national team hasn't won any major matches. But its national youth team won the world championship in 2009.

The Swiss national youth team won the world football championship in 2009. They played a team from Nigeria in the final match.

About half the Swiss people downhill or cross-country ski. Others enjoy snowboarding, bobsledding, and playing ice hockey. In summer, many people go mountain climbing, hiking, and rafting.

People of all ages enjoy downhill skiing in the Swiss Alps.

THE FLAG OF SWITZERLAND

Switzerland's flag is a bright red square with a white cross in the center. The bar going across is slightly longer than the one going up and down. It became the national flag in 1889.

FAST FACTS

FULL COUNTRY NAME: Swiss Confederation

AREA: 15,937 square miles (41,277 square kilometers), or about the same size as the states of Massachusetts and Connecticut combined

MAIN LANDFORMS: the mountain ranges Alps and Jura, the Swiss Plateau

MAJOR RIVERS: Aare, Reuss, Rhine, Rhone, and Ticino

ANIMALS AND THEIR HABITATS: alpine salamander, bearded vulture, chamois, ibex, golden eagle, lynx, marmot, mountain hare, nutcracker, and snow vole (mountains); fox, northern viper, red deer, roe deer, and squirrel (forest)

CAPITAL CITY: Bern

OFFICIAL LANGUAGES: German, French, Italian, and Romansh

POPULATION: about 7,623,400

GLOSSARY

ancestor: a relative who lived long ago

ancient: having been around for a long time; very old

capital: the city in a country or state where the government is based, or a city that is known for something in particular

continent: any one of seven large areas of land. The continents are Africa, Antarctica, Asia, Australia, Europe, North America, and South America.

glacier: a huge sheet of ice that moves slowly over land

map: a drawing or chart of all or part of Earth or the sky

mountain: a part of Earth's surface that rises high into the sky

peak: the top or highest point of a mountain

TO LEARN MORE

BOOKS

Church, Lisa R. *Heidi: Retold from the Johanna Spyri Original.* New York: Sterling, 2007. Read a shorter version of the story of Heidi.

McLuskey, Krista. *The Red Cross.* Mankato, MN: Weigl Publishers, 2003. Learn how the Red Cross started and what it does around the world.

Storrie, Paul D. *William Tell: One against an Empire.* Minneapolis: Graphic Universe, 2009. Explore the legend of William Tell through this graphic novel.

Walker, Sally M. *Glaciers.* Minneapolis: Lerner Publications Company, 2008. Learn how glaciers form and move in this book filled with full-color photos.

WEBSITES

BarenPark Bern
http://www.baerenpark-bern.ch
See the brown bears at the park in Bern.

National Geographic Kids
http://kids.nationalgeographic.com/kids/places/find/switzerland
Explore Switzerland through pictures from *National Geographic Kids.*

Swissworld
http://www.swissworld.org/en/switzerland/swiss_pics
See pictures and send your friends an e-card about Switzerland.

INDEX

The images in this book are used with the permission of: © Laura Westlund/Independent Picture Service, pp. 4 (top), 5, 44; © Gepapix/Dreamstime.com, p. 4 (bottom); © age fotostock/SuperStock, pp. 6, 28; © imagebroker.net/SuperStock, p. 7; © Nigel Ostler/Art Directors & TRIP, p. 8; © Neil Harrison/Dreamstime.com, p. 9; © Serban Enache/Dreamstime.com, p. 10; © Adina Tovy/Art Directors & TRIP, p. 11; © Elxeneize/Dreamstime.com, p. 12; © Timothy Stirling/Dreamstime.com, p. 13; The Art Archive, p. 14; © Sean Gallup/Getty Images, p. 15; © Tibor Bognar/Art Directors & TRIP, p. 16; © Mark Henley/Panos Pictures, pp. 17, 37; © Martin Ruetschi/epa/CORBIS, p. 18; © Blaine Harrington III/Terra/CORBIS, p. 19; © Adrian Moser/Bloomberg via Getty Images, pp. 20, 21; © Prisma/SuperStock, p. 22; © Sonderegger, Christof/Prisma Bildagentur AG/Alamy, p. 23; © Jennifer K. Leland, p. 24; © Benjamin Kong, p. 25; © Taylor S. Kennedy/National Geographic/Getty Images, p. 26; © Arnd Wiegmann/Reuters/CORBIS, p. 27; © Jaci Eisenberg, p. 29; © Gaetan Bally/Keystone/CORBIS, p. 30; © Stephen Lloyd Switzerland/Alamy, p. 31; © Roger T. Schmidt/Photographer's Choice/Getty Images, p. 32; © Fabrice Coffrini/AFP/Getty Images, pp. 33, 40; © Emi Cristea/Dreamstime.com, p. 34; © Hulton Archive/Getty Images, p. 35; © Catchlight Visual Services/Alamy, p. 36; © Lebrecht/The Image Works, p. 38; © BeBa/Iberfoto/The Image Works, p. 39; © Edmond Van Hoorick/SuperStock, p. 41; © Jamie McDonald/FIFA via Getty Images, p. 42; © Jan Bruder/Dreamstime.com, p. 43. Front cover: © Kristina Kolygo/Dreamstime.com.

Main body text set in Myriad Tilt 17/22. Typeface provided by Adobe Systems.